SELF-DIRECTED IRA FUNDS - MAKE MONEY
BUYING & RE-SELLING RESIDENTIAL LOTS

I0461925

BY

DANIEL CORDOBA

In Collaboration With Cindy Jackson

Co-authored by Sonia St. James

AES Education Products at IRATraining.com

Disclaimer: The book does not provide details or infer the procedure of investing, or other alternative asset investments, or other associated tax and/or legal information. If you decide to choose that investment path, we recommend that you consult with an accredited Owner Managed IRA advisor, CPA and/or legal counsel for your specific situation. This book does not promise, imply or in anyway state any level or degree of investment success.

ISBN 978-0-557-64689-0

9 780557 646890

Books in the "FROM WALL STREET TO MAIN STREET " Series

"Your Guide To Self-Directed Investing"

"How To Determine The Self-Directed IRA Or Self-Directed 401K Plan That Fits Your Needs"

"Self-Directed IRA Funds – Make Money Buying & Re-Selling Residential Lots"

Soon to be published: "How To Buy A Franchise With Your Self-Directed Retirement Funds"

VISIT **IRATRAINING.COM** FOR SELF EDUCATION GUIDES AND INFORMATION

TABLE OF CONTENTS

SECTION 1: HOW TO USE THIS BOOK

This book is intended for the individual investor who wants to manage their retirement investing using their individual retirement account (IRA or 401k). It also provides a method to determine the Owner Managed IRA investment plan that fits their needs.

Our goal is to teach you how to make money by purchasing unimproved residential lots with your retirement funds and re-selling via seller financed.

Throughout this book there is the mantra of the following benefits you will enjoy with your Owner Managed retirement account:

Absolute investment decision authority – you have Owner Managed control over your investments without custodial intervention, review fees or delays.

Checkbook control – you have the ability to write your own checks without custodial fees.

No asset value fee - you pay a fixed, small annual custodial fee regardless of your success.

Litigation protection – The LLC structure makes litigation against the retirement account very difficult.

For more information, guidance and assistance contact Asset Exchange Strategies toll free at 866.683.5228.

There are many other strategies and methods of growing your investments and you can purchase additional educational materials on Owner Managed Retirement investments at IRATraining.com

SECTION 2: BASICS OF SELF-DIRECTED IRA & 401(K) RETIREMENT PLANS

WHY THEY HAVE BECOME SO POPULAR

Self-Directed retirement plans are often referred to as 'owner managed' plans. Since 1974 a person could place real estate, notes or other non-traditional assets in their retirement. Of course, at that time almost anyone could make a decent return in the market and the perceived need for a portfolio with non-traditional assets was minimized or discouraged by traditional brokers and other professionals.

All that changed after the dot.com bomb, CEO scandals and September 11. Real estate investors were making very good profits and the stock market was floundering. People who owned real estate or had friends in real estate were looking for options to bolster badly beaten retirement accounts.

That trend has not diminished since we placed our first client in an Owner Managed IRA in 2000. After placing a multitude of Owner Managed plans, our experience is that the demand is becoming stronger.

QUESTIONS ANSWERED

How Is My Owner Managed IRA Protected If I Am Not In A Typical Wall Street Investment?

The answer is from the FDIC web site itself; "when an IRA is in a bank it is protected by the FDIC". Unlike your current situation, your IRA funds will be in a bank deposit at all times unless you choose to place them into another investment vehicle. In most cases the regular protection from the FDIC is limited to $100,000 however; Owner Managed IRAs enjoy protection up to $250,000 per account per bank. The following is directly from the FDIC web site.

What are the types of Owner Managed retirement accounts?
Types of Owner Managed retirement accounts include traditional and Roth Individual Retirement Accounts (IRAs), Simplified Employee Pension accounts, and Owner Managed Defined Contribution Plan Accounts.

How are Owner Managed retirement accounts insured?
Each person's deposits in Owner Managed retirement accounts at the same insured bank are added together and insured up to $250,000. Naming beneficiaries to an Owner Managed retirement account does not increase insurance coverage.

Are Roth IRAs treated the same as Traditional IRAs?
A Roth IRA is treated the same as a Traditional IRA for deposit insurance purposes.

So, if a depositor has both a Roth IRA and a Traditional IRA at the same insured bank, the funds in both accounts are added together and insured up to $250,000.

Here is an example:

Account Title	Account Balance
Bob Johnson's Roth IRA	$110,000.00
Bob Johnson's IRA	$75,000.00
Total	**$185,000.00**
Amount Insured	**$185,000.00**

DIFFERENCE BETWEEN TRADITIONAL SELF-DIRECTED IRA

Traditional Wall Street IRAs are generally limited to stock market investments; hence you have little control over the fluctuations of the stock market and the factors that influence it such as mergers and acquisitions, interest rates, wars, political instability, Fed Chairman's statements or policies, and Presidential campaigns. Owner Managed retirement plans allow you to make the decision what you'll invest in, and they provide you the ability to manage your chosen assets.

NEW TERMS TO LEARN

If you're investigating Owner Managed IRAs you'll need to learn the terminology. An Owner Managed IRA investment plan is an IRA program in which you as the investor direct the investment in or out of the stock market. The most popular investment is real estate. These accounts are generally administered and controlled through Owner Managed IRA custodians.

However, as you will learn in the following text you can be in complete control. A Venture™IRA LLC provides the IRA holder with many advantages: Checkbook control, Litigation protection of assets beyond state protection limitations, Ability to invest without obtaining permission, Flat custodial fees regardless of amount invested.

WHO ARE THE PLAYERS?

Custodians

In the early 2000's when Owner Managed IRAs became popular, custodians were the focal point. Their role, however, is very limited. They cannot give advice - that would constitute conflict of interest. His limitations therefore became your limitations. However, every IRA must have a custodian. Our Venture™ IRA LLC provides compliance to all the requirements yet providing you with lowest overall cost structure and control, and there are times when control means the difference between loss and gain.

Facilitators

Retirement facilitators are firms that provide a similar product to the Venture^{TM} IRA LLC but do not offer advice or ongoing support.

o Limited or No investment strategies or products. No advice offered or vested interest or obligation to you or your investment

o No implementation once you are on board

o Primarily offer checkbook control, BUT no other benefits

o Expensive, almost $500 to $1,000 more than Asset Exchange Strategies Advisors.

You can visit **IRATraining.com,** the largest education offering of Owner Managed retirement investment materials, and download self-study materials.

Attorney Groups

Traditionally expensive, complicated instruments, no investment advice, and no investment strategy offered. Most attorneys are (and should be) too busy creating instruments and therefore unable to play market detective for promising investment opportunities.

o Cost prohibitive. Your final bill could be in the tens of thousands
o Offer legal advice and the ability to gain checkbook control. It ends there
o Limited or no investment strategies
o No implementation

- It's the first one they have ever tackled; are you sure you want to risk that lack of experience?
- Success story of Starting Small & becoming very successful

In today's news we are barraged with news about the "Mortgage Meltdown" perhaps this is the perfect time for you to take advantage of a market segment that has created tremendous opportunity.

EXAMPLE INVESTOR

The following is an excerpt from Maria Fee, CEO of one of our partner companies, Remi Knox. Remi Knox specializes in notes and today in the Mortgage Meltdown they are doing a great business safely placing private money in safe private loans. This is a great example of an investment for a person who does not have the interest, time or experience to invest directly into real estate.

"As an investor I have spent a lot of time and money self-educating to understand real estate. I wanted to understand how to better control my investments instead of handing over my hard-earned savings to financial advisors who are still working to make a living. I believe in diversification like so many advisors chant.

A few years ago I was just about to buy an eight unit apartment complex. I ran my numbers, calculated my anticipated expenses and profits, made plans and knew what yield I should make from my 80-unit nest egg. What I did not plan for was a shooting that occurred on the property two weeks before I was scheduled to close on the property. That same night, 34 families moved out. Had I owned the property, I would have lost much of my anticipated yield for many, many months to come.

Regardless of my power planning, I would have little control of my financial returns in the first two years of my investment. I was back to feeling I had little or no control over my investments: I wanted safety, low risk, control, and known returns on my money. I kept studying, asking questions, seeking mentors, and finally found a well-hidden area of real estate – the notes business!

I discovered I could own the financing on a real estate transaction versus dealing with blue-collar issues such as:

o Unexpected repairs, expenses, and vacancies

o Increasing taxes

o Employee theft

o Contractor delays and cost overages, tenant

o Lawsuits

o Trash, toilets, and termites

I learned that I could use my brains not my brawn to invest in real estate. I could have collateralized investments, name my interest rate return, insure against property loss (my collateral), never received a phone call in the middle of the night, and still be diversified and invest in real estate!

Owner financing creates real estate notes. It is not a sexy investment topic but it is probably one of the most amazing financial investments we can own. This creative financing technique works in good and bad markets; rural areas and cities; and residential, land, and commercial properties. Owning the financing on the property rather than the property itself allows you to control the property without the risks, hassles, negotiations, and costs of ownership!

No banker or financial planner will tell you owner financing is a great investment. They don't get commissioned on real estate notes! Their sole purpose is to collect your money, invest it with the hopes of increasing your investment, and regardless of their success, earn commissions."

It should be noted that Maria Fee successfully grew this business from just a start up to one that was sold for a handsome profit. I personally know Maria and I believe that she would agree that most investors if they were to apply themselves could achieve the same success she achieved.

How To Know if You Are an Owner Managed Investor?

Investors have a maturation process. Just as with any other process there are certain steps and in this case there are four basic stages to an investor's development.

Advisor managed portfolios – The most basic and common form of investment is the advisor-managed portfolio. The investor for many different reasons such as time constraints or limited knowledge may not want to learn the basic skills needed to manage a portfolio. This first stage investor is reliant upon advisors and generally allows the advisor to make all the investment decisions.

Second stage, Owner Managed – This investor has taken responsibility for his portfolio and may have a basic understanding of risk management and market segments. In the world of securities investment this investor is generally with Fidelity or Charles Schwab

The successful investor at this stage has learned about macro and micro portfolio diversification. For example, an investor at this point has learned that advisor portfolio management can be very expensive. He may have learned about market segmentation and if another decline in the market should occur he knows that not all segments rise and fall at the same time.

Third stage, Owner Managed – This investor is now engaged in nontraditional markets. This requires learning how to conduct due diligence properly, the investor is now often the financier of ventures whether they are his own or other ventures. However, as with the first stage the investor still requires the need for a custodial representative and Owner Managed custodians offer the investor procedural support.

This procedural support can be very expensive and may hinder the ability to make the best deal. An example may be an investor that has moved his Owner Managed IRA away from the Owner Managed brokerage and has funds invested with an Owner Managed IRA custodian. In this case the investor has both traditional and non-traditional assets but still requires the assistance of a Owner Managed custodian.

In this stage, the custodian allows by permission for the investor to purchase an asset, the custodian holds title to the asset, the custodian charges an asset fee based on the value of the portfolio and manages the assets transactions and charges of fee for each transaction.

The biggest difference between this custodian and the traditional custodian is the allowance of non-traditional assets such as directly owning real estate. This investor is almost there but has one more stage to evolve into and that is the fourth and final stage.

Fourth stage, genuinely Owner Managed – This investor has stepped into the last and most rewarding stage. The investor now has complete control of his assets and is keeping all of the earnings by self-managing his assets. The investor's IRA operates a Venture^{TM} IRA LLC and has provided the investor with the most complete control of his destiny with the greatest return on investment.

This real estate investor may have started out with single-family units and then may have diversified into small apartments or strip centers. The single-family residence may have been the gateway to investing in real estate but the risk factors may have been higher than the investor had anticipated. A well-diversified real estate investor not only owns hard assets but also owns paper as well.

The Owner Managed investor is enjoying the following benefits:

o Absolute Checkbook Control of your IRA assets: You can write checks from your IRA with custodial-free ease.

o Investment Decision Control of Your IRA funds: You are the CEO of your financial portfolio. Get approval for your investment through a requirement-free process!

o Asset Protection through the Venture^{TM} IRA LLC: Your retirement is safeguarded from Creditors and Litigators with Comprehensive Asset Protection.

o Most Minimal Custodial Costs Offered: A once a year minimal custodial fee will keep your wallet full and will insure you are not spending your retirement years counting pennies, but counting memories.

o The Most Overall Value across the Board: You get all of the above, plus investment strategies and products that are all included. Through a network of non-traditional asset professionals.

Is an Owner Managed investment plan right for me?

Yes! If …

- You want checkbook control of your IRA;

- You want to make your own investment decisions without the need of a custodian;

- You want asset protection for your retirement beyond what is currently available;

- You want the lowest possible custodial fees;

- Find a Trusted Self Directed IRA Advisor If you're considering a self directed IRA, you need to think about:

- Finding an Advisor you are 100% comfortable with.

- If you're considering a Self-Directed IRA, you need to think about:

THE OWNER MANAGED PLAN ADVISOR

Your Owner Managed IRA investment Advisor should only deal with the IRS code and what it explicitly says. No policy interpretation, no asset fees and no requirement to report back on the desired asset purchase.

PROTECT YOURSELF FROM PROHIBITED TRANSACTIONS

An investor has the same opportunity to commit a prohibited transaction with a custodian as they would if they were on their own. Why? Because each and every custodial website states they do not and cannot offer advice. If the custodian offers advice they become liable and they'll send you back to "your" advisor for help.

If you are like most people investigating self directed IRAs you have learned that there are very few "advisors" who understand the IRA rules. We will only provide to you what the IRS says you can't do and under what circumstances. If desired, a compliance review and confirmation of correct structure will be provided.

YOU MAKE THE INVESTMENT DECISION

With custodian involvement the investment decision is theirs not yours as to what can be bought. Now the possibility of missed investment opportunity is present. Venture ^{TM} IRA LLC Advantage is you make the investment decision.

If you're not sure if it is a prohibited asset contact your Self-Directed IRA Advisor for guidance.

Assets purchased through a custodian are limited in asset protection. Venture^{TM} IRA LLC Advantage is the Venture IRA LLC^{TM} that provides asset protection for both you the IRA and the structure. Don't expect the custodian to provide any legal help or assistance. Your Advisor should be an experienced investor with a financial background.

MORE FAQ'S ON OWNER MANAGED INVESTING

Visit www.MyRealEstateIRA.com/faq

SECTION 3: DETERMINE THE PLAN THAT FITS YOUR NEEDS

Your first step is to talk to your Owner Managed Advisor who will help you to determine the plan best suited to your needs. Asset Exchange Strategies will provide you input and guidance, at no fee, to help you understand how each Owner Managed plan works and the setup process.

WHICH SELF-DIRECTED IRA PLAN IS RIGHT FOR YOU?

Now that you've defined your goal and objectives, and met with your Advisor you are ready to determine which Owner Managed investment plan is right for you.

This following graph will help you consider your investment motivators and which Owner Managed investment plan will best support them. We've also included explanation of each plan and setup process for each.

Use this graph as a guide to determine the plan that best fits your requirements.

WHAT ARE YOUR MOTIVATORS?

IF YOU REQUIRE: 
      o   Rent Income
 	
      o   Resale Income
 	
      o   Royalty Income
 	
      o   Interest Income
 	
      o   Dividends Income

THEN YOU ARE A PASSIVE INVESTOR, AND
YOUR SUITED PLAN IS AN IRA LLC

GOAL SETTING

Now that you have determined the type of Owner Managed IRA plan that fits your needs, your next step is to define what you want to accomplish with your investment plan.

The first step to starting your endeavor is to define what you want to accomplish with your Owner Managed investing plan. You will succeed and thrive much faster if you can articulate your goals, and how they will be accomplished accompanied with an action plan.

Having a clearly defined goal, and being able to articulate it will enrich the outcome when you meet with your Advisor.

If you are a serious investor, we highly recommend you write a business plan and include a well thought out financial forecast. The goal setting exercise is not meant to replace a business plan – it is merely a reference point as you get your business organized and running.

Here is a guide to set your goals and state how you will achieve them:

Goal: State the primary outcome you want to accomplish with your Owner Managed plan. Examples: o   Achieve 10-12% ROI annually

State Your Revenue Objectives: Be specific and realistic.		
Year 1 $ _____	Year 2 $ _____	Year 3 $ _____

Objectives: Write 3 key objectives that must be met in order for you to achieve your goal. Examples:
 	
   o   Set up and fund your Owner Managed IRA LLC
   o   Develop relationship with a local Real Estate Agent to locate Lots
   o   Buy undeveloped Lot(s)

When it comes to investing your retirement savings, many have learned that investing in your own endeavors will outperform mutual funds & other traditional investments.

If you have made the decision or you are considering buying and re-selling lots with your retirement funds, you will find the information here informative and helpful.

Remember, as in any new endeavor your success will depend on your ability to negotiate, stick with it attitude and activities, organization skills, and the quality of people you decide to work with.

THE IRA LLC PLAN

Your Venture™ IRA LLC allows you to use your retirement funds to invest in non-traditional investment assets including Lots and other real estate properties. This can be accomplished in these simple steps:

1. AES creates new IRA account and the Venture™IRA LLC compliant to IRS codes
   You roll-over your IRA or 401(k) to the Venture™IRA LLC
2. AES creates new bank and investment accounts at bank of your choice
3. IRA custodian buys membership in the Venture™IRA LLC
4. You direct investments and monies as the Venture™IRA LLC manager

THE PROCESS OF SETTING UP THE IRA LLC

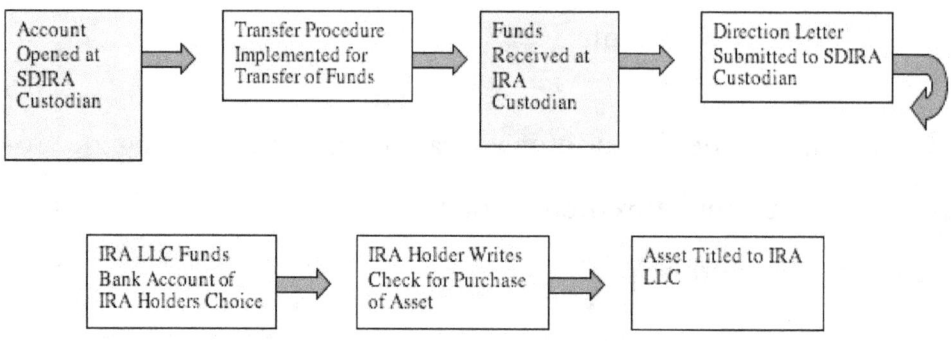

BENEFITS OF THE VENTURE^{TM} IRA LLC

Now that we have an overview of the Venture^{TM} IRA LLC let's take a look at the benefits.

Tax Deferral. The gains in the IRA continue to be deferred just as they are in a mutual funds that grows. If it is a Traditional IRA then you pay the taxes on the way out; if it is a Roth IRA then the distribution is Tax Free after all obligations have been met.

Control. You have control over the asset not a manager on Wall Street. If you need to improve the value of the property by adding a gate you can do that, you're the manager.

Value. This product is specifically designed to be used with an IRA. Unlike "me too" products the operating agreement provides protection for you and your beneficiaries if something should happen upon death or disability. Please call your Advisor and ask for the Value Proposition brochure for more details.

Experience and Understanding. Every Advisor at Asset Exchange Strategies is either a real estate investor or has a financial background.

SECTION 4: THE DEAL

INVESTING IN A LOT

There are numerous advantages to buying undeveloped Lots. It is often a hedge against the uncertainty of buying property with a pre-built structure on it.

Often Lot owners don't realize the financial potential of selling the Lot via seller financing; you can take the Lot off their hands and construct a healthy ROI for your retirement fund.

Just as in the testimonial that Maria shared, when you buy undeveloped land and resell it you don't have to deal with tenants and building maintenance. If you buy a Lot in an area that's expected to experience expanding demand in the years ahead, you'll be able to garner more when you resell it. You avoid paying the property tax out of your pocket.

Most importantly, you're able to construct your seller-financed contract to protect your interests while providing your purchaser a viable avenue of ownership. You're providing them a buying opportunity even if they are not able to obtain a traditional loan for reasons other than bad credit, such as no credit (because they have never created credit), or they do not want to deal with banks (believe it or not, there is still a sizable population that does not depend on credit lines).

We discussed the features and benefits of the IRA in both its Traditional and Roth forms; but for some investors there may be a better alternative. Just as you can contribute and self-direct investments with an IRA you are able to do the same with a 401k; to be specific the Asset Exchange Strategies Owner Managed Enterprise™401k.

The Enterprise™401k requires that the entity is an operating company. This allows the self-employed investor the opportunity to possibly expand their investment options considerably. Let's consider the features of the product and then we'll discuss the benefits of the products.

Just as with the IRA the plan document must allow for non-traditional assets and for self-direction. Checkbook control is also a necessity to be able to manage the assets.

Lets summarize the benefits that the Enterprise™401k provides:

The pre-tax contribution limits are $49,500 or $54,500 if you are over 50. The participants may also contribute up to $16,500 in the Roth account of the Enterprise 401k $16,500 or $22,500 if over 50 years of age.

There is no need for a custodian as these instruments can be self-trusted saving you more money.

If a loan is required to purchase the asset there is no Unrelated Debt Financing, which may be imposed on an IRA. This may help you increase your ability to grow your retirement dramatically.

GOING BIG

So far we have learned how an Owner Managed retirement investment plan enables you to self-direct investments on your behalf of your Owner Managed Enterprise™401k. Here are specifics to remember:

If you own and operate a company the company sponsors a 401k.

If you don't have an operating company we can help establish the needed entities.

As manager of the company, you can act as the Trustee for the plan's monies. This enables you to owner manage investments on behalf of your 401(k).

The Enterprise™401k is able to invest in traditional investments such as mutual funds if you desire.

In the pages to follow we'll demonstrate how an IRA can invest in a lot. Imagine if you could multiply the effect several time over!

How To make money on your Lot investment

By Cindy Jackson, AES Advisor

At Asset Exchange Strategies we have clients that have set up their IRA LLC and are earning 10% - 12% or more by buying rental property. Some of my clients have less than $50,000 in their IRA and are concerned with having the means to invest in real estate. This is a creative way to grow your retirement out side of the conventional way of thinking.

Myths And Truths

MYTH1: You only have $30,000 in an IRA; it is not worth the set up cost of $2,500 for an IRA LLC.

Truth1: You may not realize that the average cost of being invested in mutual funds is 4.5% a year! I have clients who have had as little as $2000 in a Roth IRA, and realized the value of the one time set up cost and how to buy real estate with a $2,000 option and turn their ROTH IRA into a $100,000 plus IRA- yes that is an exception not the rule, so we will focus on 10 -12% steady growth.

MYTH2: Creative investing ideas are always too risky. You don't have the skill I need to gain 10 -12% in my IRA.

Truth #2: There is no such thing as investing without risk. Examine the performance of your IRA or 401K over the past 10 years in the stock market if you want to get a good look at risky!

MYTH3: I need to be an expert in real estate.

Truth #3.: Just as you were not an expert at mutual funds you do not have to be an expert at real estate to buy and sell real estate. By using the expertise of a real estate professional to help you identify a good area to buy real estate for the purpose of re-selling with owner financing and then re-selling the asset for you and by utilizing a real estate attorney to prepare the proper legal documents - piece of cake!

Buy a Lot or piece of un-improved real estate and re-sell with Seller financing.

In Austin, where I am a real estate agent as well as a Self directed IRA Advisor, there are a number of unimproved lots in good re-sell areas that are under $30,000. I listed a lot near Lake Travis in an area where there is a water district, but the lots need septic.

I have the lot listed at $28,000 and I have received numerous calls from individuals seeking seller financing. These potential buyers have $5000 – $10,000 to use as down payment and good jobs, but in the current lending atmosphere, they will not qualify for a lot loan.

These buyers are willing to pay 10 – 12% interest on a 15-year note. The following information will map out the advantages of buying and re-selling Lots.

ADVANTAGES OF SELLER FINANCING

1. The buyer is responsible for all maintenance of property and all taxes.

2. If the buyer defaults – all improvements they made to the property must stay with the property and will become additional assets owned by the Seller.

3. If the buyer defaults – no return of down payment. Seller may re-sell property and retain all payments and down payment.

4. Seller may hire a "Note management company" for collection and deposit into LLC account, or choose to have payer pay directly to you to deposit in your IRA LLC account.

5. Minimize risk by using a professional real estate agent in your market or have me find you a deal here in the Austin area. After having AES set up your IRA LLC in whatever state you are in - you can buy real estate anywhere. I will be glad to coach your real estate agent and you. A real estate attorney can draw the legal documents for you.

Bottom line is that purchasing a Lot and re-selling it via seller-financed will generate for you a significant return on investment (ROI).

HOW THE PROCESS WORKS
o You have $28,850 in your IRA.

o Your real estate agent finds un-improved residential lot for $28,000 and you purchase it for this price.

o You now have your real estate agent re-list it as "seller-financed" for $32,000 with an interest rate at 10%.

o Your Lot is sold to a buyer with a down payment of $3.500.

o You have no out-of-pocket expenses since the buyer's down payment covers your closing costs.

o The buyer wants to live on the Lot: he puts a home (or mobile home) on the lot, and he improves the property by installing and paying for a septic tank (for example).

o You actually make a profit on the initial sale plus 10% monthly via the buyer's payments (normally 10% amortized over 15 years). This is 10% a year for 15 years in which the note pays $54,627.24 with $26,627.24 total in interest only.

o There is little risk involved because if the buyer defaults on the note you can re-sell the Lot for a higher price due to the improvements you had no out-of-pocket expenses for. If you are able to repeat this several times that is a darn good return!

CALCULATION - NO OUT-OF POCKET EXPENSES

Here is the example of how you have no out-of-pocket expenses with your initial Lot purchase:

NO OUT-OF-POCKET EXPENSE FOR INITIAL PURCHASE

Acquisition cost:	$28,000	
Closing Cost:	$850	(Includes new survey)
Total	$28,850	
Re-Sale Price	$33,500	
Down Payment	$3,500	(From new buyer)
Total Original Cost	$28,850	
Immediate Profit	$3,500	
Subtract Closing Cost For Re-Sell	<$3,340>	(Rounded down)
Deposit to IRA LLC	**$159**	**You realize positive cash flow on initial investment**

You finance loan for $30,000 (after down payment). See loan amortization schedule below for details on monthly cash flow earning 10%

LOAN PAYMENT SCHEDULE

Shown below are the first 24 payments on a $30,000 loan at 10% amortized for 120 months: this amortization schedule takes into consideration acquisition cost and closing cost to re-sell.

2010	Pay #	P & I Payment	Mortgage Principal Balance	Interest	Cumulative Interest
Jun	1	396.45	146.45	250.00	250.00
			29,853.55		
Jul	2	396.45	147.67	248.78	498.78
			29,705.88		
Aug	3	396.45	148.90	247.55	746.33
			29,556.98		
Sep	4	396.45	150.14	246.31	992.64
			29,406.84		
Oct	5	396.45	151.39	245.06	1,237.70
			29,255.45		
Nov	6	396.45	152.65	243.80	1,481.50
			29,102.80		
Dec	7	396.45	153.93	242.52	1,724.02
			28,948.87		
2010 Total		2,775.15	1,051.13	1,724.02	

2011	Pay #	P & I Payment	Mortgage Principal Balance	Interest	Cumulative Interest
Jan	8	396.45	155.21	241.24	1,965.26
			28,793.66		
Feb	9	396.45	156.50	239.95	2,205.21
			28,637.16		
Mar	10	396.45	157.81	238.64	2,443.85
			28,479.35		
Apr	11	396.45	159.12	237.33	2,681.18
			28,320.23		
May	12	396.45	160.45	236.00	2,917.18
			28,159.78		
Jun	13	396.45	161.79	234.66	3,151.84
			27,997.99		
Jul	14	396.45	163.13	233.32	3,385.16
			27,834.86		
Aug	15	396.45	164.49	231.96	3,617.12
			27,670.37		
Sep	16	396.45	165.86	230.59	3,847.71
			27,504.51		
Oct	17	396.45	167.25	229.20	4,076.91
			27,337.26		

			Mortgage Principal Balance		
Nov	18	396.45	168.64	227.81	4,304.72
			27,168.62		
Dec	19	396.45	170.04	226.41	4,531.13
			26,998.58		

```
                -----------------------------------------
         2011 Total    4,757.40       1,950.29    2,807.11
```

2012	Pay #	P & I Payment	Mortgage Principal Balance	Interest	Cumulative Interest
Jan	20	396.45	**171.46**	**224.99**	4,756.12
			26,827.12		
Feb	21	396.45	172.89	223.56	4,979.68
			26,654.23		
Mar	22	396.45	174.33	222.12	5,201.80
			26,479.90		
Apr	23	396.45	175.78	220.67	5,422.47
			26,304.12		
May	24	396.45	177.25	219.20	5,641.67
			26,126.87		

```
                -----------------------------------------
       2012 Total    1,982.25        871.71     1,110.54
          TOTALS     9,514.80      3,873.13     5,641.67 (In 2 years)
```

o Only the first 24 payments of 120 total payments are shown above and are included in the Grand Totals.

o Also, the first 24 payments end mid-year 2012, so the totals only include the first 5 months.

o $1,592.12 is deposited in your IRA.

o Payments begin following month at $396.45 (10% interest amortized over 10 years).

o You receive monthly payments of $396.45 / $177.78 toward principal and $219.20 toward interest.

Note: The above example is just an example — actual cost both of acquisition and re-sale may vary from state to state and local municipalities.

YOUR NOTES:

ABOUT ASSET EXCHANGE STRATEGIES, LLC

Based in Leander Texas, (near Austin), Asset Exchange Strategies offers many different opportunities to use your IRA or 401k for investment purposes; referred to as owner-managed retirement plans. They show their clients how to buy real estate, buy a business, other assets, and a host of business solutions. **Daniel Cordoba** is the principal and founder of the Asset Exchange Companies. Daniel is a featured regular speaker on Talk Radio shows as well as other financial media such as ABC World news, Wall Street Journal, Forbes, Kiplinger, Realty Times, Business Week and many other major media. He is the author of "Tax Favorable Real Estate Transactions", a course book approved by the Texas Real Estate Commission, and several books in the "From Wall Street To Main Street" series that focus on investing via Owner Managed IRA retirement plans.

Asset Exchange Strategies   www.assetexchangestrategies.com

About Purchasing Real estate   www.myrealestateira.com

Self Education Manuals/Guides   www.iratraining.com

DANIEL CORDOBA, THE AUTHOR

Principal Asset Exchange Strategies

THE RECOGNIZED KNOWLEDGE LEADER
ON ASSET EXCHANGE STRATEGIES
Online bio: danielcordoba.com

Available For:
Speaking Engagements
Seminar Programs
Personal Consultations
Executive Retirement Planning

Speaker Topics
Exercise Tax Favorable Strategies
Self-Directed Retirement Planning
Leverage Asset & Entity Advantages

Designations
B.A. in Business Management,
University of Phoenix

Professional Licenses
Texas Department of Insurance Life
and Accident Insurance, Texas Real
Estate Commission Instructor, Real
Estate Finance and Real Estate
Investments, NASD Investor Education
on Professional Designations

Contact Information
www.danielcordoba.com
info@danielcordoba.com
866-683-5228

Recognized Leader in education offerings for Owner Managed IRA Investing; Founder and President of Asset Exchange Strategies, LLC; Founder of NATFI, National Association of Tax Favorable Investing

In Detail – Daniel Cordoba is recognized as the expert in asset exchange strategies including Owner Managed retirement investing. He is quoted and featured in numerous high-end media, and continues to be sought out for speaking engagements, advice, and consulting services. He is the Author of the Texas Real Estate Commission approved real estate course: Tax Favorable Real Estate Transactions.

How He Presents – Daniel is a frequent speaker at national investor groups; an instructor to high producing real estate agents, investment talk radio shows, and television news broadcasts. His powerful presentations are packed with a rich source of actionable information, which he expresses with clarity and precision.

Media - Daniel is quoted in Kiplinger's Magazine, Wall Street Journal, Forbes, On Wall Street, Women's Wall Street, Reality Times, CPA journals and other notable online and print media.

CINDY JACKSON, COLLABORATOR

**Licensed Real Estate Agent &
Professional IRA Investor / Educator**

**Client Advocate Focusing on
IRA Real Estate Investing**

**Personal Consultations
Seminar Programs
Speaker**

Speaker Topics:

- Self-Directed Retirement
  Planning
- Leverage Asset & Entity
  Advantages

Affiliations
Connie Fuller Real Estate
Williamson County Association of
Realtors
Texas Association of Realtors,
Austin Multiple Listing Services
Asset Exchange Strategies

Professional Licenses
Texas Real Estate License

Contact Information
866-683-5228
cindy@myrealestateira.com
www.cjacksonrealty.com

In Detail

Cindy assists people to adapt and prepare for successful asset-based real estate investing.

She has twelve years experience as a licensed real estate agent, and seven years as owner and operator of Jackson and Associates Real Estate. During her career she has discovered her ability to convey how individuals can invest and leverage their assets through real estate transactions.

How Cindy Helps Her Clients
Cindy is articulate and excellence driven. She is often described with exceptional people skills and the ability to convey knowledge and concepts clearly. She is especially sensitive to other peoples needs and is a good listener, and an experienced enhancer. Her realtor background and experience provides credibility and the tangible perspective.

Because she creates order and appreciates the rhythm of business, she is sought out as a speaker and presenter.

SONIA ST. JAMES, CO-AUTHOR

MUSE TO CREATIVE MINDS

Assisting Change & Growth and Develop

Contact Information
Email:
sonia@accelerprocess.com
Phone: 512.535.3148

Author
The Handbook on Kicking The
Aging Habit™, and
Soon to be published: Preparing
For & Surviving Joint
Replacement

Co-Author
Partnering With Your IRA, and

How To Determine The Self-
Directed IRA LLC or 401(k) Plan
That Meets Your Needs

Web Sites
www.iratraining.com
www.decideonrealestate.com
www.accelerprocess.com

**Strategist, Author, Mentor,
Entrepreneur, Health/Fitness
Advocate with highly honed
collaborative and creative skills**.

St. James has extensive business
development experience including 25
years as a creative consultant, and
over 10 years assisting entrepreneurs
to grow and develop products and
services.
She is referred to as a Muse.

Founder of the AccelerProcess™
A unique method to assess, clarify
and organize your idea, challenge or
project; position it's outcome; and
develop an action plan to reach your
desired goal.

Visit AccelerProcess.com

ISBN 978-0-557-64689-0

9 780557 646890